Max,

If you want a boat you need to know this.

Get a boat.

Douglas & Mary
and all young sailors

Acknowledgement and thanks to:
Hervey Benham
John Leather
Charles & Janet Harker
Des & Liz Pawson
Nottage Institute of Boar Studies

Extract from *Swallows and Amazons*
Copyright © Arthur Ransome, 1930
Reproduced by kind permission.

© James Dodds 2000
Designed by Catherine Clark
ISBN 0 939510 73 1

Published in the United States by
Mystic Seaport Museum, Inc.
P. O. Box 6000
Mystic, CT 06355
Printed in the USA
Sixth Printing July 2013

ABC

of boat bits

**An Introduction
to Sailing a Winkle Brig**

Linocuts and Words by James Dodds

*There was a very light north-westerly
wind, brought no doubt, by the urgent
whistling of the crew. Mother held the
end of the painter, and then when the
little sail filled, she threw it to Roger
who coiled it down, and stuffed it away
under his feet. Very slowly the 'Swallow'
slid away from the jetty.*

Swallows and Amazons
by Arthur Ransome

The **Anchor** is thrown overboard to stop and hold the boat in one place. It is attached to the bow by a rope or chain.

The back of the boat is called **Aft.**

Ready ***About!*** is the command given by the helmsman just before he changes tack, when he puts the tiller over, he says *lee ho!*.

Ahoy! is shouted to attract the attention of another boat.

B

The **Boom** is a spar that holds the bottom edge of the mainsail. Care should be taken when going about or gybing that it doesn't hit you on the head.

The **Bowsprit** is the pole that sticks out at the front, the **Bow**.

The **Bobstay** is a wire from the end of the bowsprit to the lower part of the stem.

A **Block** is a block of wood plastic or metal with a wheel inside which a rope runs over, used to increase your pulling power.

The **Bailer** is for removing water from inside your boat.

Belaying Pins are used like a cleat for belaying halliards.

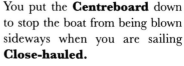

You put the **Centreboard** down to stop the boat from being blown sideways when you are sailing **Close-hauled.**

A **Cleat** is for tying off (making fast) ropes, sheets and halliards.

The **Clew** is the bottom corner of the sail nearest the sheet.

To steer a **Course** you need a fixed point. This can be a landmark, a buoy, or a star. The **Compass** is an instrument used to know which direction you are going in relative to magnetic north.

To **Capsize** is when the boat tips over and fills with water.

D

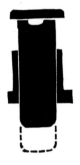

A **Daggerboard** is a centre board which is not pivoted.

Duckboards or bottom boards are what you stand on to protect the hull of the boat.

The **Draught** is the depth of the boat from the lowest point to the waterline.

*The **Devil** would have been a sailor if he'd have only looked up!* To find out which rope is which, it is best to follow the rope up to see where it goes

Davy Jones Locker is a name for the bottom of the sea, the final resting place of drowned sailors and their sunken ships.

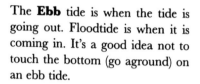

The **Ebb** tide is when the tide is going out. Floodtide is when it is coming in. It's a good idea not to touch the bottom (go aground) on an ebb tide.

The **Ensign** is the national flag.

An **Eye Splice** is a circular loop at the end of a wire or rope. Sometimes it has a metal liner inside called a cringle. A bolt fixed to the boat or mast with an eye in it is called an **Eyebolt**. Sometimes it has a wooden ring inside called a bull's eye.

The **Eye** of the wind is where the wind is coming from.

East is where the sun comes up.

F

Forward is towards the bow of the boat.

The **Forestay** is a wire stay for the mast that comes down to the end of the bowsprit or stemhead.

The bottom boards lie **Fore-and-Aft** ie in the same direction as the boat.

One **Fathom** is six feet deep.

Flags are used to see the direction of the wind and to send messages. Each letter of the alphabet has its own flag and a meaning, for example *O* means *Man Overboard!*.

The **Fender** is something hung over the side to protect the boat when going alongside.

Fairleads are fitted to the bows for taking mooring ropes.

Pennant

Throat Halliard

Forestay

JIB

Bowsprit

Bobstay

Fairleads

Anchor

Jib Sheet

Gunwale

Shroud

Centreboard

Thwart

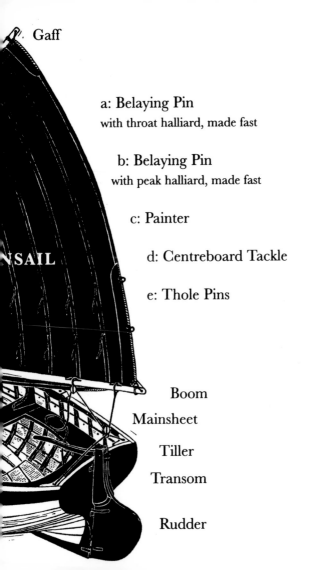

Gaff

a: Belaying Pin
with throat halliard, made fast

b: Belaying Pin
with peak halliard, made fast

c: Painter

d: Centreboard Tackle

e: Thole Pins

NSAIL

Boom

Mainsheet

Tiller

Transom

Rudder

The **Gaff** is a spar that holds the top edge of the mainsail. The highest end is called the peak and the lowest end is the throat. The gaff jaws and the boom jaws are forked ends that go either side of the mast.

The **Gunwale** is the top plank of the boat. The wale is another name for the thickest plank, and a gunwale is the plank the cannons would have poked over.

When the wind is dead behind you, the mainsail and jib can be set on opposite sides, and you are **Goosewinging**. Great care should be taken to avoid the boom swinging violently to the other side. This is a **Gybe**. You can gybe on purpose by pulling in on the main sheet to control it.

H

A **Halliard** is a rope to pull up and lower the sails. On the Winkle Brig there is the jib halliard, the throat halliard, and the peak halliard.

The **Half Hitch** is one of the most useful knots, used to secure halliards, but should never be used on sheets.

A **Hank** is a metal ring or clip which is used to secure the luff of the jib on the forestay.

When sailing close-hauled, if you pull the jib sheet to the wrong side (backing the jib), the boat will **Heave to**, or stop. This is ideal for when you have to reef the main sail in strong winds.

Inboard is the inside of the boat. Keep your fingers inboard when going alongside other boats and jetties.

When the boat faces **Into the wind** all the sails flap violently, and you go backwards. If you get stuck like this when going about, you are said to be **In Irons.**

 J

The **Jib** is the triangular shaped sail at the front. The top corner is called the head, the front edge the luff, the back edge the leech. The lower front corner is called the tack the bottom edge is called the foot, the lower aft corner is called the clew which the jib sheets are attached to.

JIB

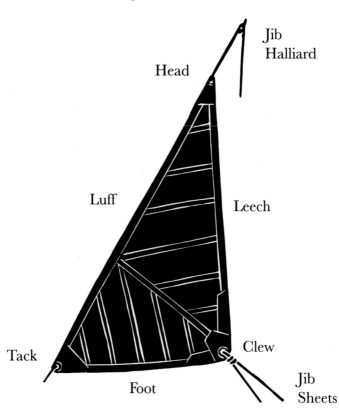

K

Kedging is a way of pulling the boat into deeper water when aground. The anchor is thrown into the water in the direction you wish to go, and the line is pulled to move the boat.

A **Knee** is wood grown to shape to form a right angle and is used to connect the thwart to the boat sides. The quarter knees join the transom to the gunwale. A breast-hook is a knee in the bows.

The **Keel** is the backbone of the boat, a long piece of timber running the whole length along the bottom of the boat.

Knots. The three most useful knots are the Reef Knot, the Bowline, and Two Half Hitches.

L

A **Lifejacket** must be worn at all times when afloat.

The **Luff** is the front edge of a sail. **Luffing up** is heading closer into the wind.

The **Lee** side is the side facing away from the wind.

A **Leadline** is a lump of lead on a rope which is marked off in fathoms. Used for measuring the depth of water, although probably not on a Winkle Brig: an oar would be enough to feel the bottom in shallow water.

Lacing is using a rope line to lace the sail to the boom, gaff or mast.

M

The **Mainsail** is the largest sail. It has a gaff lashed to the top edge, and a boom on the bottom which is sometimes also lashed. The foreward edge, the luff, is secured to the **Mast** with lacing or mast hoops. The clew of the mainsail is laced to the aftmost part of the boom. The **Mainsheet** is the rope used to control the angle of the sail. It has reefing lines which can be tied together to make the sail smaller in strong winds.

A **Marlin Spike** is used to open up rope for splicing and to tighten and undo shackles.

Mooring the boat is dropping the anchor, or tying the boat to a mooring buoy or jetty.

MAINSAIL

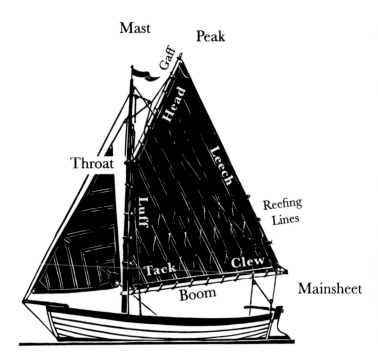

Head to Wind

Clos

Close Hauled

Close Reach

Reach

:d

Close Reach

Reach

**WIND
DIRECTION**

Broad Reach

Running

oad Reach

 **N**

Neptune is the Roman God of the sea.

When the rise and fall of the tide is at its least, it is called a **Neap** tide. This is the opposite to a Spring Tide, which is where you get the highest and lowest levels.

 O

You should always have a paddle or a pair of **Oars** on board in case you are becalmed. They are passed through rowlocks or between thole pins.

*Man **Overboard!*** means someone has fallen out of the boat!

P

The **Painter** is a short piece of rope attached to a ring in the bows used for towing or mooring the boat.

The **Peak** is the top end of the gaff. The **Peak Halliard** pulls the peak of the gaff up and down.

Port is left and red. Starboard is right and green.

The **Pennant** is the flag at the top of the mast. It shows you where the wind is coming from, which helps you to steer.

The **Planking** is the outer skin of the boat. The Winkle Brig is clinker built, where the planks overlap, a method used by the Vikings. The Romans on the other hand, favoured carvel construction where the planks butt up to each other giving a smooth hull.

The Port and Starboard **Quarters** are the left and right areas at the back of the boat.

Ahead

Starboard Bow

Port Bow

Starboard Beam

Port Beam

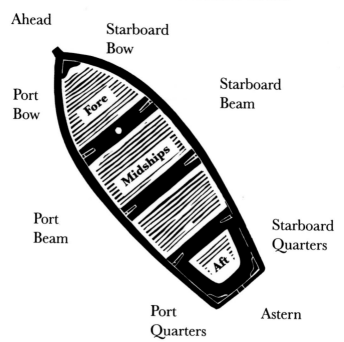

Fore

Midships

Aft

Starboard Quarters

Port Quarters

Astern

The **Rudder** steers the boat and hangs on to gudgeon pins which are like hinges on the stern of the boat. It is controlled by the tiller.

Reefing lines are tied together with a reef knot and are a way of decreasing the size of the mainsail.

Running Rigging is rigging that moves, i.e. halliards, sheets etc, as opposed to standing rigging which is shrouds and stays.

Running is sailing with the wind behind you. **Reaching** is with the wind coming from the side.

Rowlocks or thole pins in the gunwales act as pivots to heave against whilst rowing.

The **Sheets** are the ropes used to control the setting of the jib and mainsail.

Shrouds are wire **Stays** which hold the mast on either side.

Starboard is right and green. Port is left and red.

A **Shackle** is a U-shaped bit of metal closed with a pin, used in many places to join things together.

The gaff and the boom (but not the mast) are **Spars,** i.e. long round bits of wood.

Sculling is using one oar in a notch in the transom to move the boat.

Setting Sails. Steer the boat in the direction you want to go, then pull in or let out the sheets until the sail's luff has just stopped flapping. The sail is now in the best position.

T

The **Tiller** is a stick that passes through the head of the rudder and is used to steer the boat. If you push the tiller to the right, the boat will go to the left, and vice versa.

The **Tide** is the rise and fall of the sea levels as a result of what the sun and moon are doing.

The **Throat** is the end of the gaff nearest the mast, and is raised and lowered using the throat halliard.

Thwarts are the seats that run across the boat. The term **Athwartships** refers to anything across the boat (the opposite to fore-and-aft).

The **Transom** is the flat board at the stern of the boat.

Tarpaulin is the old name for a sailor or Jack Tar.

Underway means the boat is moving through the water under her own power.

Under Bare Poles means that the wind is strong enough to push you along without putting any sails up.

A Voyage is a journey undertaken at sea.

A Vang is a rope from the end of the gaff to the boat, used like a sheet on the gaff, not used on a Winkle Brig.

On the Blackwater, our boat is a **Winkle Brig,** on the River Colne it is a Bumkin. There are also variations in rig: sometimes it has no bowsprit, and a standing lugger occasionally has no jib.

The **Waterline** is the line between the bottom of the hull, and the topsides. Sometimes it is a painted line called Boot Topping.

The **Windward** side is the side where the wind is coming from, i.e. the opposite to leeward.

When there is no wind, the crew should **Whistle** up some.

The strength of the **Wind** is measured in a scale of 0 - 12 called the Beaufort Scale. Try not to be out in anything more than a 6.

Weighing Anchor is pulling the anchor up.

X marks the spot as any self respecting pirate would know.

Once you have mastered the art of sailing a Winkle Brig you may aspire to buying a **Yacht**, with a cabin, galley and pump toilet instead of a bucket.

A **Zig-Zag** is the course you take when sailing into the wind. This is called tacking to windward.

Afterword

A
B
C
D
E
F
G
H
I
J
K
L
M

This book is all about the Winkle Brig. The Winkle Brig or Bumkin is an open clinker boat with a centreboard, 15ft to 18ft long, rigged with a gaff on the mainsail and one headsail called the Jib. This rig is called a Gaff Sloop. There are several variations on this rig. One is with no bowsprit and the jib is attached to the stemhead. Another, the simplest of all is with a standing lugsail with or without a jib. The Winkle Brig is a strong forgiving work boat with a simple rig: a great boat in which to learn the rudiments of sailing.

As a young boy I learnt to sail in a Winkle Brig with my best friend and his brothers. We camped on Ray Island behind Mersea (the fictional home of Baring-Gould's *Mehalah*) and sailed out on the early morning ebb tides to explore the many veins of the creeks that intersect the marshes of the Colne and Blackwater Estuaries. Later at fifteen I was apprenticed to a boatbuilder making clinker Barge and Smack boats and the occasional Winkle Brig.

Now with children of my own, I wish to teach them to sail and to share with them the many secret places of my youth. The *Alphabet of Boats* and this book where firstly conceived as an introduction for my children to sailing and the sea.

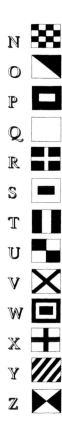